T5-AWA-746

THE FIRST ANNUAL
WHO'S IN CHARGE HERE
YEARBOOK

Gerald Gardner

A Perigee Book

For Doris Tipograph

Perigee Books
are published by
G. P. Putnam's Sons
200 Madison Avenue
New York, New York 10016

Copyright © 1981 by Gerald Gardner
All rights reserved. This book, or parts thereof,
may not be reproduced in any form without permission.
Published simultaneously in Canada by General Publishing
Co. Limited, Toronto.

Photographs courtesy of Wide World and United Press International.

ISBN 0-399-50573-3
LC 81-84762

First Perigee Printing, 1981

Printed in the United States of America

A WORD ABOUT 1981

For the planet Earth, it was a year of dramatic passage from the Age of the New Deal to the Age of the Old Movie, a time of regression and wrenching change. The pages that follow are crowded with striking images of the pleasures, pains and surprises of being alive in 1981. It was a year when an amiable actor took on the toughest job in the world, turned the economy upside down, then took the summer off. It was a year when ballplayers and air controllers struck; the first were safe, the second were out at home. A year when Israel destroyed an Iraqi reactor, Russian tanks poised on the Polish border, the medfly stung Jerry Brown, and an English girl landed an eligible Prince. It was a year when one past President disappeared into oblivion, another moved to New Jersey, and a third turned it into cash. In a world nominally at peace, there were spasms of violence. Assassins attacked a President, a Pope, and a Queen, and a headmistress killed a diet doctor. On the whole, it was better to be in Philadelphia. It was a year of spasm, shock, fear and calamity—in short, all the things that make life worth living.

—Gerald Gardner

THE FIRST ANNUAL
WHO'S IN CHARGE HERE
YEARBOOK

IRANIANS RUSH
TO MEET CARTER DEADLINE
IN FREEING HOSTAGES

POLISH UNION DEMANDS 40-HOUR WORK WEEK

ETHEL MERMAN SINGS AT REAGAN'S INAUGURAL GALA

PRESIDENT LAUGHS AT COMIC AT INAUGURAL GALA

REAGAN SWORN IN, RESOLVES TO HALT INFLATION

RAIDERS FAVORED
IN SUPER BOWL

CARTER ASSESSES REASONS FOR HIS DEFEAT

NFL SAYS OAKLAND RAIDERS MAY NOT MOVE TO L.A.

WALTER CRONKITE RETIRES FROM CBS NEWS

ARMY ISOLATES FORMER HOSTAGES AT WEST POINT

CARTER RETURNS TO WARM FAMILY HOMECOMING

FREED HOSTAGES LEAVE WEST POINT ON WAY TO WHITE HOUSE

JULIE ANDREWS EXPOSES HER BREASTS IN NEW FILM

HAIG TELLS SENATE HE NEVER MADE DEAL FOR NIXON PARDON

Let me make that perfectly clear.

NANCY ARRANGES SURPRISE PARTY FOR RONNIE'S BIRTHDAY

CALIFORNIA SUPREME COURT ENDS BUSING IN L.A.

GROUPS CHALLENGE THEORY OF EVOLUTION

REAGAN ADDRESSES NAACP

McENROE WINS AT WIMBLEDON

CONGRESSMAN SAYS BUDGET CUTS WILL HURT POOR AND HELP RICH

GOP SAYS TEDDY'S SENATE SEAT IS VULNERABLE

EX-CON, FREED BY MAILER, WANTED FOR MURDER

MAYOR KOCH SAYS HE TRAVELS IN SUBWAYS ONCE A WEEK

NIXON SELLS MANHATTAN HOUSE

REAGAN NOT AWAKENED
WITH NEWS OF DOGFIGHT

LEADERS OF AIR CONTROLLERS JAILED

ISRAELI JETS BLITZ BEIRUT

JERRY BROWN DECIDES TO CONFRONT MEDFLY THREAT

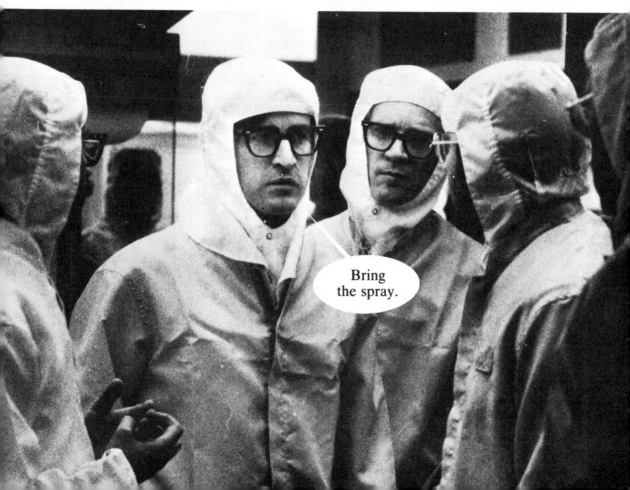

BOMB WIPES OUT 74 OF KHOMEINI'S MEN

BEGIN SENDS ISRAELI COMMANDOS INTO LEBANON

SUBSTITUTES TAKE OVER FOR AIR CONTROLLERS

REAGAN FIRES FLIGHT CONTROLLERS, SAYS SYSTEM CAN RUN WITHOUT THEM

OWNERS AND PLAYERS REACH AGREEMENT, PLAY RESUMES

AFGHANS PIN DOWN RUSSIANS

STOCKMAN TELLS SENATE AMOUNT HE WILL SPEND TO HELP THE POOR

PETER SELLERS' WIDOW MARRIES DAVID FROST

CLASH OVER MX MISSILE AND HOW TO MOVE IT AROUND

It might work.

BILLY CARTER OWES LIBYA $200,000. PAYS $1,000

STEVE AND CYNDY GARVEY ANNOUNCE SEPARATION

FORD TO EARN $900,000 BY EXPLOITING HIS PRESIDENCY

Now a word for Sara Lee.

PRESIDENT GETS LAUGHS WITH ONE-LINERS AT WHITE HOUSE

BONZO, STAR OF REAGAN FILMS, DIES

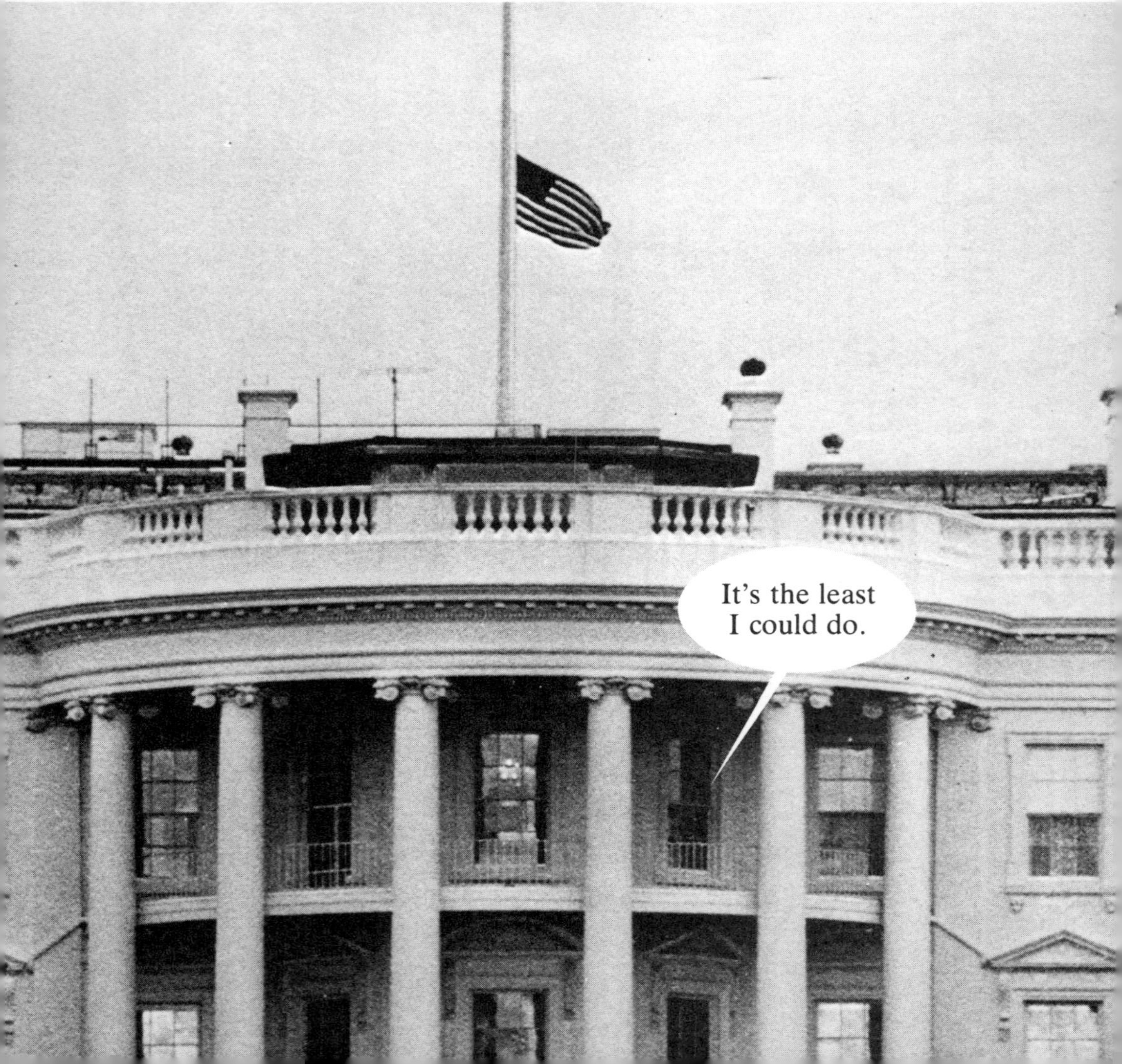

PRINCE CHARLES AND LADY DIANA LEAVE ON HONEYMOON

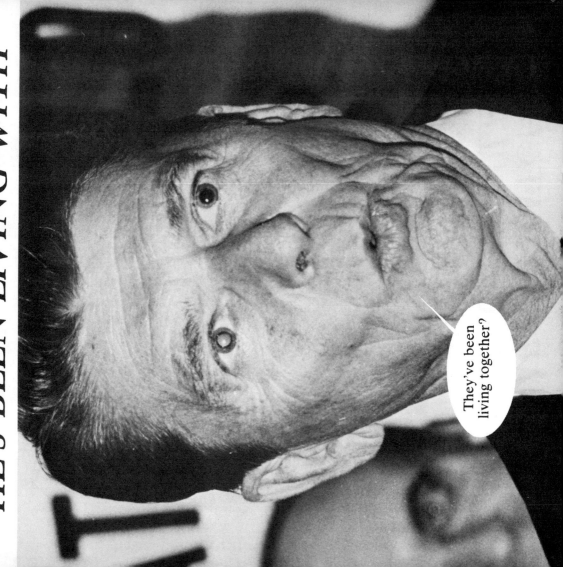

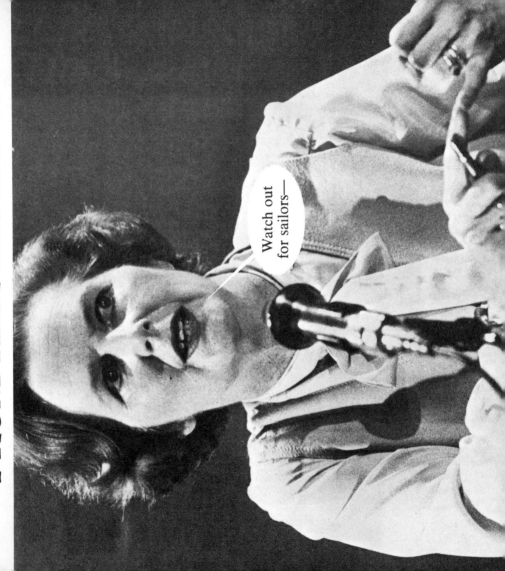

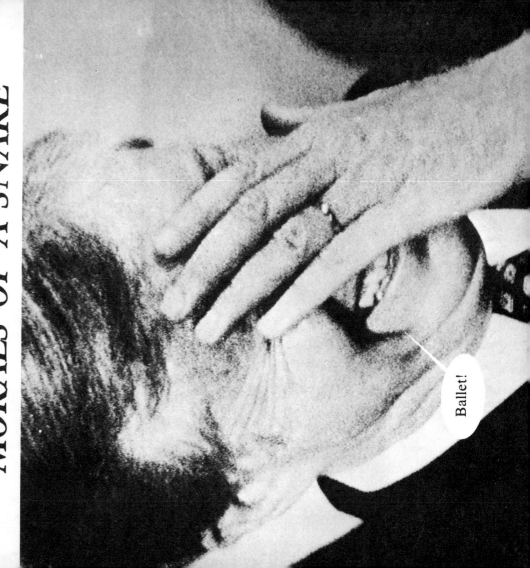